p. 13

SABBATHS

WENDELL BERRY

NORTH POINT PRESS
San Francisco 1987

Grateful acknowledgment is extended to the following publish-
ers of earlier versions of some of these poems: *The Bread Loaf
Anthology*, *Calliopea Press*, *CoEvolution Quarterly*, *Country Jour-
nal*, *Cutbank*, *Harvard Magazine*, *Journal of Kentucky Studies*,
Kentucky Poetry Review, *New England Review*, *Northern Lights*,
Ploughshares, *Temenos*, and *The Virginia Quarterly Review*.

For Donald Hall

Contents

*The whole earth is at rest, and is
quiet: they break forth into singing.*

ISAIAH 14:7

SABBATHS

1979

I

I go among trees and sit still.
All my stirring becomes quiet
around me like circles on water.
My tasks lie in their places
where I left them, asleep like cattle.

Then what is afraid of me comes
and lives a while in my sight.
What it fears in me leaves me,
and the fear of me leaves it.
It sings, and I hear its song.

Then what I am afraid of comes.
I live for a while in its sight.
What I fear in it leaves it,
and the fear of it leaves me.
It sings, and I hear its song.

After days of labor,
mute in my consternations,

I hear my song at last,
and I sing it. As we sing
the day turns, the trees move.

II

Another Sunday morning comes
And I resume the standing Sabbath
Of the woods, where the finest blooms
Of time return, and where no path

Is worn but wears its makers out
At last, and disappears in leaves
Of fallen seasons. The tracked rut
Fills and levels; here nothing grieves

In the risen season. Past life
Lives in the living. Resurrection
Is in the way each maple leaf
Commemorates its kind, by connection

Outreaching understanding. What rises
Rises into comprehension
And beyond. Even falling raises
In praise of light. What is begun

Is unfinished. And so the mind
That comes to rest among the bluebells
Comes to rest in motion, refined
By alteration. The bud swells

Opens, makes seed, falls, is well,
Being becoming what it is:
Miracle and parable
Exceeding thought, because it is

Immeasurable; the understander
Encloses understanding, thus
Darkens the light. We can stand under
No beam that is not dimmed by us.

The mind that comes to rest is tended
In ways that it cannot intend:
Is borne, preserved, and comprehended
By what it cannot comprehend.

Your Sabbath, Lord, thus keeps us by
Your will, not ours. And it is fit
Our only choice should be to die
Into that rest, or out of it.

III

To sit and look at light-filled leaves
May let us see, or seem to see,
Far backward as through clearer eyes
To what unsighted hope believes:
The blessed conviviality
That sang Creation's seventh sunrise,

Time when the Maker's radiant sight
Made radiant every thing He saw,
And every thing He saw was filled
With perfect joy and life and light.
His perfect pleasure was sole law;
No pleasure had become self-willed.

For all His creatures were His pleasures
And their whole pleasure was to be
What He made them; they sought no gain
Or growth beyond their proper measures,
Nor longed for change or novelty.
The only new thing could be pain.

IV

The bell calls in the town
Where forebears cleared the shaded land
And brought high daylight down
To shine on field and trodden road.
I hear, but understand
Contrarily, and walk into the woods.
I leave labor and load,
Take up a different story.
I keep an inventory
Of wonders and of uncommercial goods.

I climb up through the field
That my long labor has kept clear.
Projects, plans unfulfilled
Waylay and snatch at me like briars,
For there is no rest here
Where ceaseless effort seems to be required,
Yet fails, and spirit tires
With flesh, because failure
And weariness are sure
In all that mortal wishing has inspired.

10

I go in pilgrimage
Across an old fenced boundary
To wildness without age
Where, in their long dominion,
The trees have been left free.
They call the soil here "Eden"; slants and steeps
Hard to stand straight upon
Even without a burden.
No more a perfect garden,
There's an immortal memory that it keeps.

I leave work's daily rule
And come here to this restful place
Where music stirs the pool
And from high stations of the air
Fall notes of wordless grace,
Strewn remnants of the primal Sabbath's hymn.
And I remember here
A tale of evil twined
With good, serpent and vine,
And innocence as evil's strategem.

I let that go a while,
For it is hopeless to correct
By generations' toil,
And I let go my hopes and plans
That no toil can perfect.
There is no vision here but what is seen:
White bloom nothing explains.

But a mute blessedness
Exceeding all distress,
The fresh light stained a hundred shades of green.

Uproar of wheel and fire
That has contained us like a cell
Opens and lets us hear
A stillness longer than all time
Where leaf and song fulfill
The passing light, pass with the light, return,
Renewed, as in a rhyme.
This is no human vision
Subject to our revision;
God's eye holds every leaf as light is worn.

Ruin is in place here:
The dead leaves rotting on the ground,
The live leaves in the air
Are gathered in a single dance
That turns them round and round.
The fox cub trots his almost pathless path
As silent as his absence.
These passings resurrect
A joy without defect,
The life that steps and sings in ways of death.

V

How many have relinquished
Breath, in grief or rage,
The victor and the vanquished
Named on the bitter page

Alike, or indifferently
Forgot—all that they did
Undone entirely.
The dust they stirred has hid

Their faces and their works,
Has settled, and lies still.
Nobody rests or shirks
Who must turn in time's mill.

They wind the turns of the mill
In house and field and town;
As grist is ground to meal
The grinders are ground down.

VI

What stood will stand, though all be fallen,
The good return that time has stolen.
Though creatures groan in misery,
Their flesh prefigures liberty
To end travail and bring to birth
Their new perfection in new earth.
At word of that enlivening
Let the trees of the woods all sing
And every field rejoice, let praise
Rise up out of the ground like grass.
What stood, whole in every piecemeal
Thing that stood, will stand though all
Fall—field and woods and all in them
Rejoin the primal Sabbath's hymn.

VII

What if, in the high, restful sanctuary
That keeps the memory of Paradise,
We're followed by the drone of history
And greed's poisonous fumes still burn our eyes?

Disharmony recalls us to our work.
From Heavenly work of light and wind and leaf
We must turn back into the peopled dark
Of our unraveling century, the grief

Of waste, the agony of haste and noise.
It is a hard return from Sabbath rest
To lifework of the fields, yet we rejoice,
Returning, less condemned in being blessed

By vision of what human work can make:
A harmony between wood-land and field,
The world as it was given for love's sake,
The world by love and loving work revealed

As given to our children and our Maker.
In that healed harmony the world is used
But not destroyed, the Giver and the taker
Joined, the taker blessed, in the unabused

Gift that nurtures and protects. Then workday
And Sabbath live together in one place.
Though mortal, incomplete, that harmony
Is our one possibility of peace.

When field and woods agree, they make a rhyme
That stirs in distant memory the whole
First Sabbath's song that no largess of time
Or hope or sorrow wholly can recall.

But harmony of earth is Heaven-made,
Heaven-making, is promise and is prayer,
A little song to keep us unafraid,
An earthly music magnified in air.

VIII

I go from the woods into the cleared field:
A place no human made, a place unmade
By human greed, and to be made again.
Where centuries of leaves once built by dying
A deathless potency of light and stone
And mold of all that grew and fell, the timeless
Fell into time. The earth fled with the rain,
The growth of fifty thousand years undone
In a few careless seasons, stripped to rock
And clay—a "new land," truly, that no race
Was ever native to, but hungry mice
And sparrows and the circling hawks, dry thorns
And thistles sent by generosity
Of new beginning. No Eden, this was
A garden once, a good and perfect gift;
Its possible abundance stood in it
As it then stood. But now what it might be
Must be foreseen, darkly, through many lives—
Thousands of years to make it what it was,
Beginning now, in our few troubled days.

IX

Enclosing the field within bounds
sets it apart from the boundless
of which it was, and is, a part,
and places it within care.
The bounds of the field bind
the mind to it. A bride
adorned, the field now wears
the green veil of a season's
abounding. Open the gate!
Open it wide, that time
and hunger may come in.

X

Whatever is foreseen in joy
Must be lived out from day to day.
Vision held open in the dark
By our ten thousand days of work.
Harvest will fill the barn; for that
The hand must ache, the face must sweat.

And yet no leaf or grain is filled
By work of ours; the field is tilled
And left to grace. That we may reap,
Great work is done while we're asleep.

When we work well, a Sabbath mood
Rests on our day, and finds it good.

XI

To long for what can be fulfilled in time
Foredooms the body to the use of light,
Light into light returning, as the stream

Of days flows downward through us into night,
And into light and life and time to come.
This is the way of death: loss of what might

Have been in what must come to be, light's sum
Lost in the having, having to forego.
The year drives on toward what it will become.

In answer to their names called long ago
The creatures all have risen and replied
Year after year, each toward the distant glow

Of its perfection in all, glorified;
Have failed. Year after year they all disperse
As the leaves fall, and not to be denied

The frost falls on the grass as by a curse.
The leaves flame, fall, and carry down their light
By a hard justice in the universe

Against all fragmentary things. Their flight
Sends them downward into the dark, unseen
Empowerment of a universal right

That brings them back to air and light again,
One grand motion, implacable, sublime.
The calling of all creatures is design.

We long for what can be fulfilled in time,
Though death is in the cost. There is a craving
As in delayed completion of a rhyme

To know what may be had by loss of having,
To see what loss of time will make of seed
In earth or womb, dark come to light, the saving

Of what was lost in what will come—repaid
In the invisible pattern that will enark
Whatever of the passing light is made.

Choosing the light in which the sun is dark,
The stars dark, and all mortal vision blind—
That puts us out of thought and out of work,

And dark by day, in heart dark, dark in mind,
Mistaking for a song our lonely cry,
We turn in wrongs of love against our kind;

The fall returns. Our deeds and days gone by
Take root, bear fruit, are carried on, in faith
Or fault, through deaths all mortal things must die,

The deaths of time and pain, and death's own death
In full-filled light and song, final Sabbath.

XII

To long for what eternity fulfills
Is to forsake the light one has, or wills
To have, and go into the dark, to wait
What light may come—no light perhaps, the dark
Insinuates. And yet the dark conceals
All possibilities: thought, word, and light,
Air, water, earth, motion, and song, the arc
Of lives through light, eyesight, hope, rest, and work—

And death, the narrow gate each one must pass
Alone, as some have gone past every guess
Into the woods by a path lost to all
Who look back, gone past light and sound of day
Into grief's wordless catalogue of loss.
As the known life is given up, birdcall
Become the only language of the way,
The leaves all shine with sudden light, and stay.

1980

I

What hard travail God does in death!
He strives in sleep, in our despair,
And all flesh shudders underneath
The nightmare of His sepulcher;

The earth shakes, grinding its deep stone;
All night the cold wind heaves and pries;
Creation strains sinew and bone
Against the dark door where He lies.

The stem bent, pent in seed, grows straight
And stands. Pain breaks in song. Surprising
The merely dead, graves fill with light
Like opened eyes. He rests in rising.

II

The eager dog lies strange and still
Who roamed the woods with me;
Then while I stood or climbed the hill
Or sat under a tree,

Awaiting what more time might say,
He thrashed in undergrowth,
Pursuing what he scared away,
Made ruckus for us both.

He's dead; I go more quiet now,
Stillness added to me
By time and sorrow, mortal law,
By loss of company

That his new absence has made new.
Though it must come by doom,
This quiet comes by kindness too,
And brings me nearer home,

For as I walk the wooded land
The morning of God's mercy,
Beyond the work of mortal hand,
Seen by more than I see,

The quiet deer look up and wait,
Held still in quick of grace.
And I wait, stop footstep and thought.
We stand here face to face.

III

Great deathly powers have passed:
The black and bitter cold, the wind
That broke and felled strong trees, the rind
Of ice that held at last

Even the fleshly heart
In cold that made it seem a stone.
And now there comes again the one
First Sabbath light, the Art

That unruled, uninvoked,
Unknown, makes new again and heals,
Restores heart's flesh so that it feels
Anew the old deadlocked

Goodness of its true home
That it will lose again and mourn,
Remembering the year reborn
In almost perfect bloom

In almost shadeless wood,
Sweet air that neither burned nor chilled
In which the tenderest flowers prevailed,
The light made flesh and blood.

IV

The frog with lichened back and golden thigh
Sits still, almost invisible
On leafed and lichened stem,
Invisibility
Its sign of being at home
There in its given place, and well.

The warbler with its quivering striped throat
Would live almost beyond my sight,
Almost beyond belief,
But for its double note—
Among high leaves a leaf,
At ease, at home in air and light.

And I, through woods and fields, through fallen days
Am passing to where I belong:
At home, at ease, and well,
In Sabbaths of this place
Almost invisible,
Toward which I go from song to song.

V

Six days of work are spent
To make a Sunday quiet
That Sabbath may return.
It comes in unconcern;
We cannot earn or buy it.
Suppose rest is not sent
Or comes and goes unknown,
The light, unseen, unshown.
Suppose the day begins
In wrath at circumstance,
Or anger at one's friends
In vain self-innocence
False to the very light,
Breaking the sun in half,
Or anger at oneself
Whose controverting will
Would have the sun stand still.
The world is lost in loss
Of patience; the old curse
Returns, and is made worse
As newly justified.

In hopeless fret and fuss,
In rage at worldly plight
Creation is defied,
All order is unpropped,
All light and singing stopped.

VI

The intellect so ravenous to know
And in its knowing hold the very light,
Disclosing what is so and what not so,

Must finally know the dark, which is its right
And liberty; it's blind in what it sees.
Bend down, go in by this low door, despite

The thorn and briar that bar the way. The trees
Are young here in the heavy undergrowth
Upon an old field worn out by disease

Of human understanding; greed and sloth
Did bad work that this thicket now conceals,
Work lost to rain or ignorance or both.

The young trees make a darkness here that heals,
And here the forms of human thought dissolve
Into the living shadow that reveals

All orders made by mortal hand or love
Or thought come to a margin of their kind,
Are lost in order we are ignorant of,

Which stirs great fear and sorrow in the mind.
The field, if it will thrive, must do so by
Exactitude of thought, by skill of hand,

And by the clouded mercy of the sky;
It is a mortal clarity between
Two darks, of Heaven and of earth. The why

Of it is *our* measure. Seen and unseen,
Its causes shape it as it is, a while.
O bent by fear and sorrow, now bend down,

Leave word and argument, be dark and still,
And come into the joy of healing shade.
Rest from your work. Be still and dark until

You grow as unopposing, unafraid
As the young trees, without thought or belief;
Until the shadow Sabbath light has made

Shudders, breaks open, shines in every leaf.

1981

Here where the world is being made,
No human hand required,
A man may come, somewhat afraid
Always, and somewhat tired,

For he comes ignorant and alone
From work and worry of
A human place, in soul and bone
The ache of human love;

He may come and be still, not go
Toward any chosen aim
Or stay for what he thinks is so.
Setting aside his claim

On all things fallen in his plight,
His mind may move with leaves,
Wind-shaken, in and out of light,
And live as the light lives,

And live as the Creation sings
In covert, two clear notes,
And waits; then two clear answerings
Come from more distant throats—

May live a while with light, shaking
In high leaves, or delayed
In halts of song, submit to making,
The shape of what is made.

1982

I

Dream ended, I went out, awake
To new snow fallen in the dark,
Stainless on road and field, no track
Yet printed on my day of work.

I heard the wild ones muttering,
Assent their dark arrival made
At dawn, gray dawn on dawn-gray wing
Outstretched, shadowless in that shade,

Down from high distances arrived
Within the shelter of the hill;
The river shuddered as they cleaved
Its surface, floated, and were still.

II

Here where the dark-sourced stream brims up,
Reflecting daylight, making sound
In its stepped fall from cup to cup
Of tumbled rocks, singing its round

From cloud to sea to cloud, I climb
The deer road through the leafless trees
Under a wind that batters limb
On limb, still roaring as it has

Two nights and days, cold in slow spring.
But ancient song in a wild throat
Recalls itself and starts to sing
In storm-cleared light; and the bloodroot,

Twinleaf, and rue anemone
Among bare shadows rise, keep faith
With what they have been and will be
Again: frail stem and leaf, mere breath

Of white and starry bloom, each form
Recalling itself to its place
And time. Give thanks, for no windstorm
Or human wrong has altered this,

The forfeit Garden that recalls
Itself here, where both we and it
Belong; no act or thought rebels
In this brief Sabbath now, time fit

To be eternal. Such a bliss
Of bloom's no ornament, but root
And light, a saving loveliness,
Starred firmament here underfoot.

III

The pasture, bleached and cold two weeks ago,
Begins to grow in the spring light and rain;
The new grass trembles under the wind's flow.
The flock, barn-weary, comes to it again,
New to the lambs, a place their mothers know,
Welcoming, bright, and savory in its green,
So fully does the time recover it.
Nibbles of pleasure go all over it.

IV

Thrush song, stream song, holy love
That flows through earthly forms and folds,
The song of Heaven's Sabbath fleshed
· In throat and ear, in stream and stone,
A grace living here as we live,
Move my mind now to that which holds
Things as they change.
                          The warmth has come.
The doors have opened. Flower and song
Embroider ground and air, lead me
Beside the healing field that waits;
Growth, death, and a restoring form
Of human use will make it well.
But I go on, beyond, higher
In the hill's fold, forget the time
I come from and go to, recall
This grove left out of all account,
A place enclosed in song.
                          Design
Now falls from thought. I go amazed
Into the maze of a design

That mind can follow but not know,
Apparent, plain, and yet unknown,
The outline lost in earth and sky.
What form wakens and rumples this?
Be still. A man who seems to be
A gardener rises out of the ground,
Stands like a tree, shakes off the dark,
The bluebells opening at his feet,
The light one figured cloth of song.

V

To Mary

A child unborn, the coming year
Grows big within us, dangerous,
And yet we hunger as we fear
For its increase: the blunted bud

To free the leaf to have its day,
The unborn to be born. The ones
Who are to come are on their way,
And though we stand in mortal good

Among our dead, we turn in doom
In joy to welcome them, stirred by
That Ghost who stirs in seed and tomb,
Who brings the stones to parenthood.

VI

To Den

We have walked so many times, my boy,
over these old fields given up
to thicket, have thought
and spoken of their possibilities,
theirs and ours, ours and theirs the same,
so many times, that now when I walk here
alone, the thought of you goes with me;
my mind reaches toward yours
across the distance and through time.

No mortal mind's complete within itself,
but minds must speak and answer,
as ours must, on the subject of this place,
our history here, summoned
as we are to the correction
of old wrong in this soil, thinned
and broken, and in our minds.

You have seen on these gullied slopes
the piles of stones mossy with age,
dragged out of furrows long ago

by men now names on stones,
who cleared and broke these fields,
saw them go to ruin, learned nothing
from the trees they saw return
to hold the ground again.

But here is a clearing we have made
at no cost to the world
and to our gain—a *re*-clearing
after forty years: the thicket
cut level with the ground,
grasses and clovers sown
into the last year's fallen leaves,
new pasture coming to the sun
as the woods plants, lovers of shade,
give way: change made
without violence to the ground.

At evening birdcall
flares at the woods' edge;
flight arcs into the opening
before nightfall.

Out of disordered history
a little coherence, a pattern
comes, like the steadying
of a rhythm on a drum, melody
coming to it from time
to time, waking over it,

as from a bird at dawn
or nightfall, the long outline
emerging through the momentary,
as the hill's hard shoulder
shows through trees
when the leaves fall.

The field finds its source
in the old forest, in the thicket
that returned to cover it,
in the dark wilderness of its soil,
in the dispensations of the sky,
in our time, in our minds—
the righting of what was done wrong.

Wrong was easy; gravity helped it.
Right is difficult and long.
In choosing what is difficult
we are free, the mind too
making its little flight
out from the shadow into the clear
in time between work and sleep.

There are two healings: nature's
and ours and nature's. Nature's
will come in spite of us, after us,
over the graves of its wasters, as it comes
to the forsaken fields. The healing
that is ours and nature's will come

if we are willing, if we are patient,
if we know the way, if we will do the work.
My father's father, whose namesake
you are, told my father this, he told me,
and I am telling you: we make
this healing, the land's and ours:
it is our possibility. We may keep
this place, and be kept by it.
There is a mind of such an artistry
that grass will follow it,
and heal and hold, feed beasts
who will feed us and feed the soil.

Though we invite, this healing comes
in answer to another voice than ours;
a strength not ours returns
out of death beginning in our work.

Though the spring is late and cold,
though uproar of greed
and malice shudders in the sky,
pond, stream, and treetop raise
their ancient songs;
the robin molds her mud nest
with her breast; the air
is bright with breath
of bloom, wise loveliness that asks
nothing of the season but to be.

VII

The clearing rests in song and shade.
It is a creature made
By old light held in soil and leaf,
By human joy and grief,
By human work,
Fidelity of sight and stroke,
By rain, by water on
The parent stone.

We join our work to Heaven's gift,
Our hope to what is left,
That field and woods at last agree
In an economy
Of widest worth,
High Heaven's Kingdom come on earth.
Imagine Paradise.
O dust, arise!

VIII

Our household for the time made right,
All right around us on the hill
For time and for this time, tonight,
Two kernels folded in one shell,

We're joined in sleep beyond desire
To one another and to time,
Whatever time will take or spare,
Forest, field, house, and hollow room

All joined to us, to darkness joined,
All barriers down, and we are borne
Darkly, by thoroughfares unsigned
Toward light we come in time to learn,

In faith no better sighted yet
Than when we plighted first by hope,
By vows more solemn than we thought,
Ourselves to this combining sleep

55

A quarter century ago,
Lives given to each other and
To time, to lives we did not know
Already given, heart and hand.

Would I come to this time this way
Again, now that I know, confess
So much, knowing I cannot say
More now than then what will be? Yes.

May 29, 1957
May 29, 1982

IX

(Sunday, July 4)

Hail to the forest born again,
that by neglect, the American benevolence,
has returned to semi-virginity, graceful
in the putrid air, the corrosive rain,
the ash-fall of Heaven-invading fire—
our time's genius to mine the light
of the world's ancient buried days
to make it poisonous in the air.
Light and greed together make a smudge
that stifles and blinds. But here
the light of Heaven's sun descends,
stained and mingled with its forms,
heavy trunk and limb, light leaf and wing,
that we must pray for clarity to see,
not raw sources, symbols, worded powers,
but fellow presences, independent, called
out of nothing by no word of ours,
blessèd, here with us.

X

The dark around us, come,
Let us meet here together,
Members one of another,
Here in our holy room,

Here on our little floor,
Here in the daylit sky,
Rejoicing mind and eye,
Rejoining known and knower,

Light, leaf, foot, hand, and wing,
Such order as we know,
One household, high and low,
And all the earth shall sing.

1983

I

In a crease of the hill
under the light,
out of the wind,
as warmth, bloom, and song
return, lady, I think of you,
and of myself with you.
What are we but forms
of the self-acknowledging
light that brings us
warmth and song from time
to time? Lip and flower,
hand and leaf, tongue
and song, what are we but welcomers
of that ancient joy, always
coming, always passing?
Mayapples rising
out of old time, leaves
folded down around
the stems, as if for flight,
flower bud folded in
unfolding leaves, what

are we but hosts
of times, of all
the Sabbath morning shows,
the light that finds it good.

II

The year relents, and free
Of work, I climb again
To where the old trees wait,
Time out of mind. I hear
Traffic down on the road,
Engines high overhead.
And then a quiet comes,
A cleft in time, silence
Of metal moved by fire;
The air holds little voices,
Titmice and chickadees,
Feeding through the treetops
Among the new small leaves,
Calling again to mind
The grace of circumstance,
Sabbath economy
In which all thought is song,
All labor is a dance.
The world is made at rest,
In ease of gravity.
I hear the ancient theme

In low world-shaping song
Sung by the falling stream.
Here where a rotting log
Has slowed the flow: a shelf
Of dark soil, level laid
Above the tumbled stone.
Roots fasten it in place.
It will be here a while;
What holds it here decays.
A richness from above,
Brought down, is held, and holds
A little while in flow.
Stem and leaf grow from it.
At cost of death, it has
A life. Thus falling founds,
Unmaking makes the world.

III

Now though the season warms
The woods inherits harms
Of human enterprise.
Our making shakes the skies
And taints the atmosphere.
We have ourselves to fear.
We burn the world to live;
Our living blights the leaf.

A clamor high above
Entered the shadowed grove,
Withdrew, was still, and then
The water thrush began
The song that is a prayer,
A form made in the air,
That all who live here pray,
The Sabbath of our day.

May our kind live to breathe
Air worthy of the breath
Of all singers that sing

In joy of their making,
Light of the risen year,
Songs worthy of the ear
Of breathers worth their air,
Of makers worth their hire.

IV

Who makes a clearing makes a work of art,
The true world's Sabbath trees in festival
Around it. And the stepping stream, a part
Of Sabbath also, flows past, by its fall
Made musical, making the hillslope by
Its fall, and still at rest in falling, song
Rising. The field is made by hand and eye,
By daily work, by hope outreaching wrong,
And yet the Sabbath, parted, still must stay
In the dark mazings of the soil no hand
May light, the great Life, broken, make its way
Along the stemmy footholds of the ant.
    Bewildered in our timely dwelling place,
    Where we arrive by work, we stay by grace.

1984

I

Over the river in loud flood,
in the wind deep and broad
under the unending sky, pair
by pair, the swallows again,
with tender exactitude,
play out their line
in arcs laid on the air,
as soon as made, not there.

II

A tired man leaves his labor, felt
In every ligament, to walk
Alone across the new-mowed field,
And at its bound, the last cut stalk,

He takes a road much overgone
In time by bearers of his name,
Though now where foot and hoof beat
stone
And passed to what their toil became,

Trees stand that in their long leaf-fall,
Untroubled on forgiving ground,
Have buried the sledged stone with soil
So that his passing makes no sound.

He turns aside, and joins his quiet
Forebears in absence from that way.
He passes through the dappled light
And shadow that the breeze makes sway

Upon him and around him as
He goes. Within the day's design
The leaves sway, darkly, or ablaze
Around their edges with a line

Of fire caught from the sun. He steps
Amid a foliage of song
No tone of which has passed his lips.
Watching, silent, he shifts among

The shiftings of the day, himself
A shifting of the day's design
Whose outline is in doubt, unsafe,
And dark. One time, less learned in pain,

He thought the earth was firm, his own,
But now he knows that all not raised
By fire, by water is brought down.
The slope his fields lie on is poised

Above the river in mere air,
The breaking forewall of a wave,
And everything he has made there
Floats lightly on that fall. To save

What passes is a passing hope
Within the day's design outlawed.
His passing now has brought him up
Into a place not reached by road,

73

Beyond all history that he knows,
Where trees like great saints stand in time,
Eternal in their patience. Loss
Has rectified the songs that come

Into this columned room, and he
Only in silence, nothing in hand
Comes here. A generosity
Is here by which the fallen stand.

In history many-named, in time
Nameless, this amplitude conveys
The answering to the asking rhyme
Among confusions that dispraise

The membering name that Adam spoke
By gift, and then heard parcelled out
Among all fallen things that croak
And cry and sing and curse and shout.

The foliage opens like a cloud.
At rest high on the valley side,
Silent, the man looks at the loud
World: road and farm, his daily bread,

His beasts, his garden, and his barns,
His trees, the white walls of his house,
Whose lives and hopes he knows. He yearns
Toward all his work has joined. What has

He by his making made but home,
A present help by passing grace
Allowed to creatures of his name
Here in this passing time and place?

III

The crop must drink, we move the pipe
To draw the water back in time
To fall again upon the field,
So that the harvest may grow ripe,
The year complete its ancient rhyme
With other years, and a good yield
Complete our human hope. And this
Is Sunday work, necessity
Depriving us of needed rest.
Yet this necessity is less,
Being met, not by one, but three.
Neighbors, we make this need our feast.

IV

The summer ends, and it is time
To face another way. Our theme
Reversed, we harvest the last row
To store against the cold, undo
The garden that will be undone.
We grieve under the weakened sun
To see all earth's green fountains dried,
And fallen all the works of light.
You do not speak, and I regret
This downfall of the good we sought
As though the fault were mine. I bring
The plow to turn the shattering
Leaves and bent stems into the dark,
From which they may return. At work,
I see you leaving our bright land,
The last cut flowers in your hand.

V

Estranged by distance, he relearns
The way to quiet not his own,
The light at rest on tree and stone,
The high leaves falling in their turns,

Spiralling through the air made gold
By their slow fall. Bright on the ground,
They wait their darkening, commend
To coming light the light they hold.

His own long comedown from the air
Complete, safe home again, absence
Withdrawing from him tense by tense
In presence of the resting year,

Blessing and blessed in this result
Of times not blessed, now he has risen.
He walks in quiet beyond devision
In surcease of his own tumult.

1985

I

Not again in this flesh will I see
the old trees stand here as they did,
weighty creatures made of light, delight
of their making straight in them and well,
whatever blight our blindness was or made,
however thought or act might fail.

The burden of absence grows, and I pay
daily the grief I owe to love
for women and men, days and trees
I will not know again. Pray
for the world's light thus borne away.
Pray for the little songs that wake and move.

For comfort as these lights depart,
recall again the angels of the thicket,
columbine aerial in the whelming tangle,
song drifting down, light rain, day
returning in song, the lordly Art
piecing out its humble way.

Though blindness may yet detonate in light,
ruining all, after all the years, great right
subsumed finally in paltry wrong,
what do we know? Still
the Presence that we come into with song
is here, shaping the seasons of His wild will.

II

A gracious Sabbath stood here while they stood
Who gave our rest a haven.
Now fallen, they are given
To labor and distress.
These times we know much evil, little good
To steady us in faith
And comfort when our losses press
Hard on us, and we choose,
In panic or despair or both,
To keep what we will lose.

For we are fallen like the trees, our peace
Broken, and so we must
Love where we cannot trust,
Trust where we cannot know,
And must await the wayward-coming grace
That joins living and dead,
Taking us where we would not go—
Into the boundless dark.
When what was made has been unmade
The Maker comes to His work.

III

Awaked from the persistent dream
Of human chaos come again,
I walk in the lamed woods, the light
Brought down by felling of great trees,
And in the rising thicket where
The shadow of old grace returns.
Leaf shadows tremble on light leaves,
A lighter foliage of song
Among them, the wind's thousand tongues,
And songs of birds. Beams reaching down
Into the shadow swirl and swarm
With gleaming traffic of the air,
Bright grains of generative dust
And winged intelligences. Among
High maple leaves a spider's wheel
Shines, work of finest making made
Touchingly in the dark.
                              The dark
Again has prayed the light to come
Down into it, to animate
And move it in its heaviness.

So what was still and dark wakes up,
Becomes intelligent, moves, names
Itself by hunger and by kind,
Walks, swims, flies, cries, calls, speaks, or sings.
We all are praising, praying to
The light we are, but cannot know.

IV

The fume and shock and uproar
of the internal combustion of America
recede, the last vacationers gone
back to the life that drives away from home.

Bottles and wrappers of expensive
cheap feasts ride the quieted current
toward the Gulf of Mexico.

And now the breeze comes down
from the hill, the kingfisher returns
to the dead limb of the sycamore,
the swallows feed in the air
over the water.
           A muskrat draws his V
under the lowhanging willows.
In clear shallows near the rocks
tiny fish flicker and soar. A dove
sweetens the distance with his call.

Out of the frenzy of an August Sunday
the Sabbath comes. The valley glows.
A raincrow flies across the river
into the shadowy leaves. The dark falls.

V

How long does it take to make the woods?
As long as it takes to make the world.
The woods is present as the world is, the presence
of all its past, and of all its time to come.
It is always finished, it is always being made, the act
of its making forever greater than the act of its destruction.
It is a part of eternity, for its end and beginning
belong to the end and beginning of all things,
the beginning lost in the end, the end in the beginning.

What is the way to the woods, how do you go there?
By climbing up through the six days' field,
kept in all the body's years, the body's
sorrow, weariness, and joy. By passing through
the narrow gate on the far side of that field
where the pasture grass of the body's life gives way
to the high, original standing of the trees.
By coming into the shadow, the shadow
of the grace of the strait way's ending,
the shadow of the mercy of light.

Why must the gate be narrow?
Because you cannot pass beyond it burdened.
To come into the woods you must leave behind
the six days' world, all of it, all of its plans and hopes.
You must come without weapon or tool, alone,
expecting nothing, remembering nothing,
into the ease of sight, the brotherhood of eye and leaf.

VI

Life forgives its depredations;
new-shaped by loss, goes on.
Luther Penn, our neighbor
still in our minds, will not
come down to the creek mouth to fish
in April anymore. The year
ripens. Leaves fall. In openings
where old trees were cut down,
showing the ground to the sky,
snakeroot blooms white,
giving shine unto the world.
Ant and beetle scuttle through
heroic passages, go to dust;
their armor tumbles in the mold.
Broad wings enter the grove, fold
and are still, open and go.

VII

The winter wren is back, quick
Among the treeroots by the stream,
Feeding from stem to stone to stick,
And in his late return the rhyme

Of years again completes itself.
He makes his work a kind of play.
He pauses on a little shelf
Of rock, says "Tick!" and flirts away,

Too busy in that other world
His hungry vision brings to sight
To be afraid. He makes a gnarled
Root graceful with his airy weight,

Breathes in the great informing Breath,
Made little in his wing and eye,
And breathes it out again in deft
Bright links of song, his clarity.

1986

Slowly, slowly, they return
To the small woodland let alone:
Great trees, outspreading and upright,
Apostles of the living light.

Patient as stars, they build in air
Tier after tier a timbered choir,
Stout beams upholding weightless grace
Of song, a blessing on this place.

They stand in waiting all around,
Uprisings of their native ground,
Downcomings of the distant light;
They are the advent they await.

Receiving sun and giving shade,
Their life's a benefaction made,
And is a benediction said
Over the living and the dead.

In fall their brightened leaves, released,
Fly down the wind, and we are pleased
To walk on radiance, amazed.
O light come down to earth, be praised!

Notes

1983

III   *line 24: Luke 10:7.*

1984

II   *line 10: George Herbert, "Love (I)," line 3.*

1985

VI   *line 11: Psalm 97:4 (The Book of Common Prayer).*
VII   *line 13: Job 34:14–15.*